New Orleans Courtyards and Gardens

The Knapp Press
PUBLISHERS

New Orleans Courtyards and Gardens
was created and produced by
REBUS, INC.
and published by THE KNAPP PRESS
5900 Wilshire Boulevard
Los Angeles, California 90036

ISBN 0-89535-155-2

In the Vieux Carré—the French Quarter—of New Orleans, along the streets that preserve the houses from the early part of the nineteenth century (and a few from the eighteenth), iron gates and barred doors and archways offer constantly recurring glimpses into a world of carefully nurtured intimate gardens: a world of privacy at once revealed and reserved.

The way back into this private domain, through the gates and archways, is marked occasionally by a gas lamp or an iron bell— and, within the passageway, by a stairway that leads up and off to what may have been slave quarters or the garret of a French pirate. On through the passageway may be another gate, or doors leading on to other doors, until at last one emerges in a courtyard, surrounded on four sides by high walls. The courtyard is filled with vines, plants set out in what were once great olive-oil jars, hedges, palm and ba-nana trees—and, more than that, little pools, statues of cherubs, fantastic iron griffins clinging to the rims of small fountains.

The most powerful impression of these hidden gardens is of green: the green of boxwood, the green of wisteria, the green of sweet olive and of aspidistra.

Around the walls of the gardens are balconies, trellises, ironwork—all covered with hanging baskets and climbing vines. And, although the enduring impression is of shades of green, there are other colors as well: red, pink, coral, and white azaleas, camellias, magnolias, night-blooming jasmine, oleander, pomegranates, kumquat and lemon trees, dwarf oranges, Japanese plum, and strawberries. New Orleans is a tropical hothouse, and things grow in profusion and fill the courts with fragrances.

These private retreats from the world are like nothing so much as informal outdoor living rooms, often furnished with cool iron furniture: places to take morning coffee or petit déjeuner, to have a candlelit dinner or a soi-ree. Originally many of these retreats were not laid out as courtyards but as carriageways and as working areas, where servants could wash and hang clothes and prepare food near kitchens out back. New Orleanians eventually came to see these utilitarian spaces as precious and turned them into courtyards.

For much of its history, New Orleans was a hot, damp, muddy, unpaved city, whose in-habitants cast their garbage and sewage into the streets. Those who sought respite from the city turned inward, to their private, walled, and sweet-smelling gardens.

These gardens are called both courtyards (from the French *cours*) and patios (from the Spanish), although, strictly speaking, the two are not the same. Courtyards are larger than patios, are bounded by high walls, and have carriage entrances or wide corridors leading to them from the street. Patios are often com-pletely enclosed inner spaces, entered through the house or sometimes by way of a small side entryway. Both are paved with flagstones or bricks. (The bricks, usually laid in a herringbone pattern, sometimes as many as four layers deep over the soggy ground, provided solid paving for horse and carriage.) They are precisely and tidily designed little spaces. The ideal of the French garden is everywhere evident: the hedges are placed just so, the walkways set down in basic geometries, the trees and plants set out with a highly refined sense of order. And yet the climate is such, and the vegetation, and the nature of things, that the vines and flowers cannot be entirely civilized; they are lush, luxuriant, almost wild. New Orleans was once a great cypress swamp, and the heat and humidity and rich soil still conspire to produce an astonishing variety of plants and flowers, from evergreens to tropical palms, shrubs, herbs, vines, oaks draped with Spanish moss, pond lilies, and the ever-present oleander.

Elsewhere in New Orleans there are larger gardens, to be sure—in the Garden District and off such tree-lined boulevards as Esplanade Avenue and surrounding the plantation houses around Bayou St. John. The older, more traditional, of these gardens favor jasmine, camellias, magnolias; the more recently planted gardens are perhaps more colorful, with their roses, irises, azaleas, lilies, and poinsettias (sometimes found blooming in the summer).

When the Garden District was originally laid out in the 1830s, the entire neighborhood seemed a vast, continuous garden, with the houses set in among the plantings. The largest of the gardens, then as now, were consciously refined landscape architecture, with arbors and hedgerows leading to entries beneath columned porticoes—miniature gardens of Fontainebleau and Versailles, geometrically exact, severely pruned, somewhat pretentious in fact, with their elaborate gazebos and pavilions, and altogether formal. They are beautiful and planted with beautiful green and flowering things; they are the public aspect of New Orleans: polite, civil, refined. They are not the lush, luxuriant, wild gardens of the courtyards and patios—where New Orleans still nurtures the pleasures of private life.

A PORTFOLIO OF
NEW ORLEANS COURTYARDS AND GARDENS

———

Impatiens, flanking an iron gate, greet those seeking a secluded, shady spot for afternoon refreshment. The garden suite includes chairs gathered around a table set with more of the bright flowers. Among the dense plantings are pear, orange, and kumquat trees.

Once a carriageway, this courtyard on Ursulines Street is dense with azaleas of white, pink, and coral. Gardenias, in bloom at least twice a year, add their strong fragrance to the garden. The brick herringbone floor is four layers deep—strong support for carriages and wagons. The brick wall, more than forty feet high, is the exterior of the neighboring house.

Alone in an arbor of white flowering vines, a stone goddess appears as a shrine—a classical setting that encourages contemplation in an intimate New Orleans garden.

A beloved Southern flower, the camellia gives New Orleans its first—and most famous—winter blooms. The tender green shrubs produce many-petaled blossoms ranging in color from red to white.

Here on a grand scale are all the elements of an elegant New Orleans courtyard: fountain, cool cast-iron furniture, marble statuary, exuberant plant life. In addition to azaleas there are Japanese wisteria and an abundance of vines. Dr. Joseph Montegut, a surgeon, built the house in 1795 and often entertained in this courtyard—among his guests were royal exiles from the French Revolution.

Ferns, growing in pots and from cracks and crevices, ascend a narrow stairway in a tiny walled garden in the heart of the French Quarter. Wisteria—all green here, but lavender in bloom—makes a sort of garland along the handrail. Nearly unnavigable for the plants, the stairs lead to the roof of the courtyard's carriage house.

Oleanders are abundant in New Orleans and here they reach to the top of an iron lamp. The bushes' evergreen leaves grow in whorls on long branches that bear little blossoms of white and shades of pink and purple. Shivering in mild breezes, even the largest specimens seem delicate. The beauty and fragility of the oleander are for the eyes only—every part of the plant is poisonous.

Brick walkways radiate from an octagonal pool in one of the French Quarter's larger, shady courtyards. The beds are given over to expanses of grass and other green plantings. Pink caladiums color the foreground, while the white variety are tucked along the garden's walls.

A calla lily sprouts from a little pool in the bricked courtyard of the Soniat House, built in 1830. Lilies and palmettos bank the pool, which is fed by water trickling from a dolphin into a constantly overflowing shell basin. The courtyard, both sunny and shady, is home to an array of green and flowering plants—and goldfish.

A great arch opens onto elegant landscaping in a courtyard built in 1792 by a Spanish military leader. Central to the courtyard's pleasures is a large Japanese plum, a springtime vision with dark green leaves and yellow fruit. Like many New Orleans courtyards, this one was originally conceived as a carriageway and workspace.

Infinitely discreet, this courtyard is double chambered: the foreground garden, accessible only through a sidewalk gate, is an anteroom to another beyond. In pots and raised brick beds, the halved courtyard hoards impatiens, water hyacinths, ferns, and pink caladiums.

All white and green—and formal in design—this large garden on Ursulines Street seems ready for the arrival of a wedding party in morning clothes. Magnolia trees shade the periphery of the geometrically arranged beds, defined with boxwood and filled with white azaleas. Potted white chrysanthemums circle the fountain.

Thriving in New Orleans' tropical climate, a banana tree, here in detail, grows in a small walled garden off Ursulines Street in the French Quarter. The pendulous, ruddy bloom is the tree's male flower; the green "fingers" are female—and they will grow and ripen into the yellow fruit.

In New Orleans' uptown Garden District, grassy pathways lie beyond an ornate cast-iron balcony railing. Though the roomy garden makes an overall impression of green—particularly the green of boxwood—roses and azaleas add extravagant splashes of color. Such well-ordered, richly appointed landscapes as this one gave the Garden District its name.

14

A classically inspired pavilion rises above great mounded boxwoods in the formal garden from the immediately preceding pages. The small pool in the foreground adds to the stately yet tranquil scene.

CREDITS

All photography by Barbara S. Harvey except for cover and numbers 9, 14, and 15 by Paul Rocheleau; numbers 1 and 10 by Alan Karchmer; and number 8 by Pierre de La Barre

The Editors would like to thank the following for their assistance: Mrs. Genevieve Munson Trimble; The Garden Study Club of New Orleans; New Orleans Spring Fiesta Association.

Picture Editor: Mary Z. Jenkins; Editor: Vance Muse; Designer: Ronald Gross; Production: Paul Levin; Managing Editor: Fredrica Harvey